FIND YOUR
KILLER IDEA

The Essential Guide To Discover
The Right Business

By TIM COOLEY

Author: Tim Cooley
Title: FIND YOUR KILLER IDEA
Subtitle: The Essential Guide To Discover The Right Business
ISBN: 9781793863423
Category: Business, Entrepreneurship

Publisher: Tim Cooley

....

DEDICATION

I always tell people, "If the people around you don't want you to succeed, you won't." Fortunately, I have surrounded myself with many people who want and encourage me to succeed.

I want to thank you all for encouraging me and believing in me. Especially to my family, you mean the world to me and I would be nothing without your constant support. To my friends Jared, Jackson, Rick and Binoy you will never know how much I thrive on your wisdom and drive.

FIND YOUR KILLER IDEA

The Essential Guide To Discover The Right Business

By TIM COOLEY

CONTENTS

INTRODUCTION

I cannot promise this book will make you millions, but I can promise to provide a clear path to take the *right* idea from conception to market viability.

By researching the myriad of business ventures--both successful and unsuccessful--my clients have undertaken in the past, I have determined a four-step process to help you know if an idea is "killer."

You have one job as a founder of a business; You have to leverage your available resources to serve your customers and be profitable. Success like this can be accomplished by anyone, if you are honest with yourself and follow my four-step process.

In this book, not only will you learn to recognize your current resources and start down the path to leveraging them, but you will find useful tools to help identify and filter your ideas. You will learn some key questions to ask yourself about your capability to execute your idea. You will learn ways to test your assumptions. You will also start spotting when it is a good time to kill an idea and when it is time to keep pushing forward. Most importantly, you will learn how to identify a Killer Idea.

I started my first "business" when I was a seven-year-old in Katy, Texas, a small town just outside Houston. My house was about a five-minute walk from a bayou, but the local swimming pool was our major form of summer entertainment. I wanted a Nintendo Entertainment System more than anything in the world--like most kids at the time.

I decided the best way to raise the money was to sell wrapping paper door-to-door in my neighborhood. Through hard work, perseverance, and a little pity from kindly neighbors for my adorable, pleading eyes, I earned enough to spend the winter playing Zelda.

Later, in middle school, I moved to Pittsburgh. I did not give up my drive for entrepreneurship; I shoveled driveways, mowed lawns and took on a paper route. In high school, I moved to Eugene, Oregon. I continued a paper route as well as helped develop a promotions company, which marketed the high school auditorium for community use. After that, I joined the Marine Corps. Following that I earned a degree from Northern Arizona University.

Through it all, I had the itch to really *do something*. My first tech venture started during my first Master's Degree in Salt Lake City, Utah, in 2009. I built an online exercise rewards platform, which I ultimately sold. After that, I spent three years in online marketing, working for hundreds of local and national companies. In 2013, I earned an MBA focusing on innovation and entrepreneurship and ran a milestone based investment fund providing over $300,000 in seed funding to hundreds of companies.

Since then, I have helped would-be founders turn ideas sketched on napkins into million-dollar companies. I have consulted and coached entrepreneurs from Denmark, Columbia, Italy and South Korea, helping create opportunities for them to do business in the United States. As an entrepreneur-in-residence at an incubator in Salt Lake City, I coached, mentored and advised thousands of entrepreneurs in ideation, product development, marketing, sales and operations. I have raised capital, lead highly skilled teams to launch products, and worked on many creative and interesting ideas, as well as a few awful ones, some of which are covered in this book. I have seen many thunderous successes and plenty of abysmal failures.

All of these experiences helped shape not only the person and businessman I am today, but the book in your hands. By reading it, I am hoping my wide range of experiences will help you look at business opportunities differently, see them more practically, and a have a process whereby you are able to analyze whether an idea is killer or should be killed.

FOUR STEPS TO A KILLER IDEA

I am going to share with you a proven process that has taken me over 10 years to develop. The secret formula I will be sharing with you is like something you have never seen before. It is not a conventional way to look at business and business opportunities. In fact, it takes what is normal and flips it. In my process we start from the bottom, the outcome we do not really want, and we work backward to become successful. From here on out the way you look at ideas will be forever changed, for the better.

Let us get right to it. There are four steps in the *killer ideas* process: **Create**, **Discover**, **Build**, and **Test.**

Create: You need an idea.
Discover: Learn as much as you can about the resources needed to deliver the idea.
Build: Make one.
Test: Sell it.

Killing an idea is not a progressional step, but a mentality that is present throughout the four-step process. In my experience, the two most important steps in this process are *Discover* and *Build*. Entrepreneurs often do not spend enough time on these, to their own disservice. If you want to learn how to save money developing and testing your idea, spend time in those two sections. I go into great detail to help shine light on areas that are often overlooked with ideas that should be killed

KILLING AN IDEA

I mentioned before that we are going to flip the script when it comes to idea development. This means that you cannot be afraid to kill an idea. Let us not get confused by terminology. We are in the pursuit of a killer idea and to do that we may have to kill a few ideas along the way.

Killing an idea is not a step but a mentality. You should constantly be in kill seeking mode early in the process. You have to be willing to walk away from your baby. This is unconventional thinking. Every other book and seminar will try to teach you how to make your idea successful, this book focuses on you and your ability to leverage available resources.

You are looking for red flags, and major roadblocks that you cannot overcome without some type of intervention outside your control. Once you realize this you will also recognize that killing an idea is not a bad thing. In fact, it can be a great thing. As an entrepreneur, you are constantly developing resources that you can use to your advantage. Just because an idea is killed does not mean it is not valuable. The resources you have gained in developing that idea are still available for you to leverage on the next idea.

Killing an idea also does not mean it is dead dead. Sometimes it just needs time. Have you ever had that one problem you could not really solve, then you go for a walk or have an interesting dream and "bam" you have the answer? This can also happen with business ideas, as you will see in one of my examples, Our First Quilt, later in the book.

Do not kill an idea too early, but also do not be afraid to kill an idea. There are plenty of ideas that are right for you. Let us find those!

KILLER IDEA

We have talked about killing an idea and that will come up many times throughout the process, but the reason you are here is to find a *Killer Idea*. Because we are looking for that killer idea it is important to recognize how ideas can present themselves.

I truly believe that there is no such thing as a bad idea. However, working on just a "good" idea and not a killer idea can lead to a very bad situation, financially, emotionally and physically.

Good ideas usually feel nice, but are ultimately unsuccessful. A good idea will present itself in one of two ways:

1) You spend a lot of money making the idea real, but cannot bring the product to market or find out no customer will actually buy it.
2) You know how to bring the product to market and have customers waiting, but you do not have access to the resources to make it a reality.

In both of these cases, you will never see your product or service fully realized.

What we want are *killer* ideas. A killer idea is one that maximizes your resources. If your idea is HUGE and your access to resources is small, there is no way you will ever be successful in this venture, so kill it. If the resources you have access to match the resources needed for this venture, your likelihood for success exponentially improves! I cannot say this enough, a killer idea maximizes your existing resources. Therefore, a killer idea looks like this:

1) You completely bring the idea to market with the resources you have.
2) You find someone who is willing to pay for it.

Unfortunately, many entrepreneurs have too many "good" ideas that can be costly and frustrating to work on before ultimately failing; I want to help you discover if your idea is killer.

The reason why many children entrepreneurs have lemonade stands is because it is a killer idea. These children have access to water, lemons, sugar, cups and investors (their parents.) These young entrepreneurs leverage those resources to go out and make money. It may seem simple, but all successful entrepreneurs share in this ability to leverage their available resources. Recognizing available resources and leveraging them is not easy and is the reason I developed my four-step process.

"

A Killer Idea is an idea:

1) You completely bring the idea to market with the resources you have.
2) You find someone who is willing to pay for.

"

STEP 1: CREATE

We are naturally creative. We like making things. It makes us feel good to use our hands and minds to create something into existence.

This is true for entrepreneurs, especially first time entrepreneurs. Unfortunately, inexperienced entrepreneurs do not enjoy spending time in the details needed to make an idea killer and jump right into the *Build* phase of their idea. I am not implying that building your idea is a mistake, necessarily, but if we take a step back, we will realize that by spending more time in the *Create* and *Discover* phases we may save ourselves tremendous amounts of money and time.

Caveat: If you are still working on your *first* idea, you get a free pass to not follow my process completely. I still highly recommend going through the process, but the amount of knowledge you will gain by building is irreplaceable. Put your heart into your idea and do everything you can to make it a reality!

IDEATION

This may seem obvious, but all businesses start with an idea. Crazy as it sounds, I have met many "entrepreneurs" who do not actually have an idea for a *business*. These people are in love with idea of entrepreneurship and being their own boss one day. Regardless if you are new to entrepreneurship or seasoned at coming up with ideas there are, essentially, only two ways to start a business. One way is to come up with something completely original. The second way is to springboard off an existing idea. You can take a product or service you know well and make it better and more valuable. Both are perfectly acceptable. It bears repeating that it is totally acceptable to use an existing idea or business model. In fact, if this is your first venture, I encourage you to do something similar to what someone else is doing while trying to make it better. Keep in mind the ethical and legal limitations of cloning a business model, product, or other intellectual property.

"

Two ways to generate ideas:

1) Come up with something completely original.
2) Innovate on an existing idea or model

IDEA

Every business idea is a solution to a problem, or a product or service that provides pleasure. A solution-based business is one that directly solves a problem a customer has. A pleasure-based business is one where the customer is buying something because it makes them feel a certain way or are looking to feel a certain way. Google, for example, is a solution to needing to search the internet for information. Facebook is a solution to connecting people. A baseball game is a service that provides pleasure. You may like baseball or want to take your child to a game, because this purchase makes you feel good. A video game is a product that provides pleasure. We are going to use the word "idea" to represent a solution-based business or pleasure-based business.

"

Every business is a product or service that either solves a problem or provides pleasure to a customer.

PROBLEM-SOLUTION FIT

So, how do you start? How do you actually come up with an idea? Often--too often--you may hear questions like those below when asked to help develop an idea:

What are you passionate about?
What one problem in the world would you fix?
What gets your blood boiling?
What problem do you want to solve?

There is one fundamental issue with these questions: they do not completely address *value.* Thy deal only with the business concept known as "Problem-Solution Fit." Questions like these assume that consumers only buy products if they solve a problem, which is not always true. It is my belief that consumers make purchases thanks to a combination of *problem, value* and *emotion.* The questions above can help start the ideation journey. They do not get at what it truly takes to get a consumer to pull out their wallet and spend their money, the second half of creating a killer idea.

"

Purchases are made when you find the right combination of problem, value and emotion.

"

THE PROBLEM WITH PROBLEM

Think about the last thing you bought. What problem did it solve? Let us assume you bought a toothbrush. What problem would that have solved? My guess would be an issue with oral hygiene. Nevertheless, did you buy a buy a basic toothbrush or an electric one? Is there any other way to keep your teeth clean other than a toothbrush? Yes, there are many ways. You chose to buy a toothbrush instead. Why? If the mission were only to keep your teeth clean, then you would have selected the cheapest option. However, this may not be the case. What are the other factors at play? It is these factors that add to the value and are the reason why don't always buy the cheapest option.

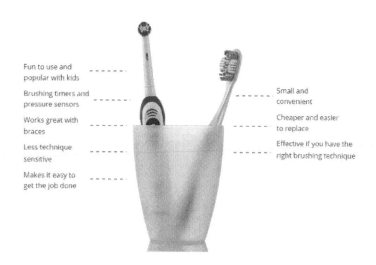

Fun to use and popular with kids

Brushing timers and pressure sensors

Works great with braces

Less technique sensitive

Makes it easy to get the job done

Small and convenient

Cheaper and easier to replace

Effective if you have the right brushing technique

EXERCISE

Think about all the t-shirts you own. Did you buy them to keep you from being naked? Odds are, you own more than a handful. Mentally list as many as you can, then answer this question: what problem does a t-shirt literally solve? Clearly, you bought each one for a reason; do all of them solve the same problem? Do some of them solve any problem at all? Why did you buy them? What was it about the "non-problem" t-shirts that motivated you to buy them? Did you buy one when you visited Disney World with your family? Were any of the shirts free, or given out as, for example, as a prize for taking part in a marathon? Or was every t-shirt you bought simply to prevent you from being naked or cold?

It is likely you can see where this is going. Each t-shirt you purchased had some value associated with it outside of "a garment that prevents me being naked". Some of the t-shirts may represent a good memory; others may have been funny or interesting; many are given as an add-on or bonus gift when you made a purchase, like a running event. Think about the t-shirts as you develop your ideas; solving your nakedness problem is not the only reason you bought them. No more focusing on

"Problem-Solution Fit". From here on, we focus on creating value, otherwise known as "Value Creation."

CREATING VALUE

What is value? Value is the worth or usefulness a consumer gives to our products or service. Therefore, the value of your product must be equal to or greater than the amount of money a customer is willing to spend. If you have ever looked at a product and said, "Oh wow, that's expensive," it means your willingness to pay for that product was lower than the listed price. On the flipside, if you ever said, "Oh wow, that's a bargain," you believe the value the product created was worth more than the price tag. As you work on your product to determine the value your it produces, it is your mission to ensure the customer does not have either of those responses. It all depends on your strategy, but if a common saying with your product is that it is cheap, you may be leaving money on the table. Ideally, you want the cash value to be equal or slightly above the value of your product or service.

How do you create value? There are four components to value creation: Economical, Functional, Social and Psychological Value. All successful business ventures take advantage of one or more of these components when creating value. Economical and Functional values are *quantitative*, easily measured and compared with other objective data. Social and Psychological values are *qualitative*, they are more personal, flexible, subjective, and more difficult to measure.

Let us break these value components down further, and then look at a few examples.

ECONOMICAL VALUE

Economical value is probably the simplest of value components to determine. It asks, "Can your product or service save time or money over the competition?" If your product is cheaper and provides the same service, then it is economically better and thus more valuable. By the same metric, if you can save your customers time your product is thus more valuable. Those are straightforward concepts. Walmart is a great example of a price-based value creation business. Roomba, the automatic vacuum, is an example of time-based value creation.

Another component of economic value is geographic location. Not every pizza place in your city delivers to your neighborhood, so you order from the ones who do. Value is not created because it is cheaper or because it saves time, but purely based on the location. Thus, all other value components come secondary to geographic location availability. This type of value is extremely common in service-based industries such as food service and delivery, cleaning and landscaping, automotive, and even medical services.

"

Economical value answers the question 'Can your product or service save time or money over the competition?'

"

FUNCTIONAL VALUE

Functional value is often what we think about when we start a business. Functional value answers the question *"What does this product or service do?"*

An idea can be like a Swiss Army Knife, and come with many different features, or it can be more like a nine-inch high-quality chef's knife that is exceptional at doing exactly one thing. Functions are often referred to as the *features* or *different services offered*. Deciding what function to offer seems like a simple task, but this component of value creation is where early entrepreneurs often make mistakes.

In some cases, being extremely good at one thing is not good enough to compete against your direct competition. For example, Omlet initially launched as a social media platform with a key feature of communicating with customizable stickers. Unsurprisingly, most people have never heard of Omlet, as the concept was just a minor feature when compared to Facebook. Since launch they have pivoted to be a platform for live streaming games.

Applying the concept of functional value, imagine building software that would compete against Indeed, the careers-search website. First, the software would require numerous features just to be on par with what Indeed already offers. After equality is achieved, you would have to add something more. What core feature would you create to add more value to your product to attract customers away from your competitor and onto your platform? How would you communicate that feature?

Functional value is not only customer specific, but is also industry and product/service-specific. If you are focusing strictly on functional value, it can be challenging to persuade people that your idea is better than another already-established one. For example, if you were wanting to create a shoe brand. How would you pull customers away from Nike?

"

Functional value answers the question 'What does your product or service do?'

SOCIAL VALUE

Social value has to do with the way one is perceived. Social value asks the question "How does this product or service make me look to others?" Social Value can be considered a modifier of status. Imagine you are waiting in line to attend a lecture on killer ideas in entrepreneurship and the speaker pulls up to the curb in a brand new cherry-red Ferrari. Many people would automatically assume the speaker was highly successful and that the talk automatically had merit because he or she had "made it" and was clearly financially successful. What if, later, you found out the speaker had rented the car? Many people would accuse that person of being a fraud. Ethical or not, companies often try to make their product appeal toward a certain demographic based purely on improving perceptions of social status or providing a sense of belonging. Companies such as Gucci, Coach, Boss, and Porche are examples of companies which have successfully created "in" groups by providing the perception of a premium product and communicating individual wealth. Although a community centered on "wealth" is often the avenue companies take to achieve this, it is certainly not the only way. Most products attempt to communicate the idea of belonging to some kind of collective, which is why the word "family" is so commonly used by brands.

Another form of status is education. The title of *Doctor of Philosophy*, or *PhD,* indicates more knowledge than a Master's, Bachelor's or Associate's Degree. Educational titles carry social currency. Degrees are products, which customers, (students) and employers place value on.

Creating social value is challenging, but when done right it can have a positive impact on the success of your idea.

"

Social value often answers the question 'How does this product or service make me look to others?'

"

PSYCHOLOGICAL VALUE

Psychological value comprises the *emotional* component of a purchase and answers the question "How does this product make me feel when I buy it?" It comes into play either when there is no other reason to purchase the item or when all other reasons are secondary. TOMS is a great example of a shoe company that provides extremely high psychological value. Customers do not typically buy TOMS shoes because they are the most functional shoe on the market, nor the least expensive, but because they love the fact that there is a social cause associated with their purchase. In this case buying the product makes one feel part of an action for social change, giving the customer a feeling of well-being.

Psychological and physical arousal, such as those associated with feelings of fear or the potential for sex, have similar emotional responses. In his book *Predictably Irrational*, Dan Ariely illustrates that human beings' ability to make rational decisions is impaired when we are aroused. We see this not only in consumer product marketing, but also from television and print news sources which play on fear to create perceived value. It is much easier to manipulate a consumer into buying a product if you can instill an emotional response such as fear in combination with (or instead of) delineating its benefits. Skin care companies execute this constantly by convincing consumers that members of the opposite sex won't find an individual as attractive if that individual fails to use their product(s); this is much more effective than claiming a product simply does A, B and C.

Other products that capitalize on psychological value are books, movies, video games and other forms of expression and entertainment. Companies have to create value by appealing to consumers' feelings in order to motivate the purchase.

"

Psychological value often answers the question 'How does this product make me feel when I buy it?'

VALUE GRAPH

Where does your idea fit?

Functional Value

What Do You Do?
Features
Specific Function

Social Value

Status (Rolls Royce)
Status (Health)
STatus (PHD)

Economical Value

Save Money?
Save Time?
Location?

Psychological Value

How Do I Feel?
Arousal
Pleasure

EXAMPLES OF IDEA,

PROBLEM AND VALUE

Write your ideas down! I cannot emphasize this enough. Many entrepreneurs keep an idea diary, including myself. The main goal of an idea diary is to have a place to start. From here, you can start exploring each idea. We are going to start with value, but you will quickly expand this to resources needed to execute once we get into the Discovery process. I recommend organizing your idea diary with these categories: Idea, Problem and Value to start.

The following are examples of how you could organize your idea diary based on real world products.

FIDGET SPINNER

FIDGET SPINNER

Idea: A device that spins in circles that you can hold between your fingers

Problem: Help people with ADHD focus.

Value:
Economical: ??
Functional: Anecdotal data suggests helping with anxiety and a number of other issues, including ADHD.
Social: It is cool to have and cool to be seen with.
Psychological: ??

Notes:
In many of my presentations, I ask, "How many of you in this room own a fidget spinner?" About 30% of the room will raise their hand. The follow-up question, "How many of you with your hands raised have been diagnosed with ADHD?" Almost every hand goes down. Therefore, I ask, "If products and services only exist to solve problems, why did anyone other than those with ADHD have a fidget spinner?

A fidget spinner might have started by solving a problem, but the real market value ended up being in the social value it created, it was cool.

PINATAGRAM

Your Message
Here!

PINATAGRAM

Idea: Send a little nine-inch donkey piñata filled with candy through the mail to cheer someone up, deliver an invitation, or just send a friendly message.

Problem: People need to send messages to one another.

Value:
Functional: Piñatagrams are often used in place of letters for invitations.
Economical:??
Social: It has a strange appeal when other see you get this random present.
Psychological: Getting a letter in the mail is always fun, but getting a donkey filled with sweets is so much cooler.

Notes: There is more qualitative value created with this product than quantitative. It is exciting to get one and turns heads. Try sending one of these, the reaction is amazing.

BURGER

BURGER

Idea: Put some ground beef between some bread

Problem: Hunger

Value:
Functional: ??
Economical: ??
Social: ??
Psychological: ??

Notes: Notice how the value in this product is unknown. This is because there are tons of ways to compete in an industry like food.

Yes, food solves a very basic need. I would argue that every single person who reads this book could successfully start a burger joint. There are probably quite a few within a mile or two of where you live or work. So how do they compete? If they were all just solving a problem, then in a competitive market, economics would dictate only one would be successful. However, burger joints compete more according to a qualitative value than quantitative value. Some burger places offer a tastier product, and others are for specific demographics, like vegans and vegetarians, while others focus on proximity to high-volume business traffic, *i.e.* being close to places where many people live or work.

My goal is to show you that while the entrepreneur theory focuses on the narrow question "what problem are you solving?" *you* should focus on the broader question of how to create real value; solving a problem is only one component of value creation.

"

Solving a problem is only one component of value creation.

EXERCISE

Grab an object within arm's reach. It could be a remote control, blanket, sock, alarm clock; anything you like. Would it be possible to create a product that solves the same problem and compete in the market with a new value proposition? Could it be even better at one specific task, or do more tasks than the original? Could it be made more cheaply? Could owners of this product belong to a common group or class? Could it be cool or exclusive? Could it be combined with or take advantage of a social cause?

CONVEY VALUE

No matter what business you are in, every business is in the business of marketing and sales. This means the value you convey has to persuade a consumer to *buy*.

This is no easy feat. Often, maybe too often, the value we are creating seems obvious to us, but the words we use to convey that value does not translate to the consumer. In addition, we are asking the consumer to change a learned or ingrained behavior, which is difficult for anyone to achieve; if you have ever tried to lose weight, you know how tough this can be. Keep this in mind when you convey the value your product or service brings to your customer.

If you are struggling with ways to convey value, try answering these three questions:
1) What is the main job that your product or service is trying to perform?
2) How does it intend to make the consumer feel?
3) What will the consumer get out of using your product or service?

Once you have this written down, make 50 variations of the same idea or pick different features to focus on, and then test them by talking to people.

KILLING AN IDEA

Creating value is the first step in the ideation process. This step is free, so spend time thinking about all of the different ways you can create value; even small permutations in approach can reap superior results. At this stage in the process, we do not know if our idea is killer; in fact, we will not truly know whether our idea is killer until Step 5 in the process. You have to be honest with yourself in your ability to create and convey value to the consumer; if you cannot create value with your idea, kill it.

STEP 2: DISCOVER

I hope you spent some quality time in the *Create* step. By now, you should have figured out a way to add value to your idea. You still do not know how well your idea translates to your customers. Before we move on to *Build* or *Test* the idea we need to spend time with Step 2: *Discover*.

Discover means "to find (someone or something) unexpectedly or in the course of a search". I prefer the term "discover", rather than "learn", because the process of discovery leaves room for spontaneity and serendipity--what happens when things come together, seemingly without planning, whether by raw fortune, unfailing ambition, or a little of both. Discovery allows synchronicity to occur. When we want to know something specific, we just Google a question to find the answer, but when setting out on a process of discovery, anything can trigger a thought that we need to dive deeper in and explore more, leading us to new, exciting, and potentially profitable places.

Entrepreneurs should be constant learners, so this step requires you to push yourself beyond what you currently understand to be true of the world. As the expression goes, "You do not know what you do not know." An entrepreneur needs to overcome this and aim to know everything about everything pertaining to their idea. It is imperative you know your customers intimately. What do they like and how do they behave? You need to know the market place. You need to know how to get your product in front of those customers at the right time with the right message. You need to know how to build your product, the processes and the nuances. Obviously, there may always be things you can't know immediately, but through this process, you can Discover critical aspects of the idea that may help you discern its quality and longevity; ultimately, the *Discover* step is the most vital when it comes to understanding whether your idea is *killer* or should be killed.

"

Discover means 'to find (someone or something) unexpectedly or in the course of search.

IDEATION

This is the fun part. Dream big. If you could build the best version of your idea possible, what would it look like? What features would it have? We will not be building this unrealistic version, but it helps to discover the most important elements of the idea you need to Build. It is better to have a ton of ideas and let customers filter them out now, than it is to just add a bunch of ideas during the Build step, known as scope creep. Scope creep is bad, really bad!

Some products *seem* straightforward, but do not let yourself get too closed-minded. Discovery is about being open to all ideas and listening in strange places, like the mall, church, restaurant, watching an ad or attending a seminar. You are not actively seeking solution from any specific source. Instead you are passively seeing how new ideas might apply to your business. It is important to document these discoveries as they can lead to new and better ideas. This skill takes practice. Learn to sit on things a little longer than you want to. Never give up on crazy; use it to find out what is important. Whenever I start a new project, I write down every possible result. I think, if this thing were to go huge, what else would I need in terms of building the product, marketing, sales, personnel, etc? This important part of the discovery phase will help avoid tunnel vision. Be sure to write these ideas down. The list will become a starting point to better understand what the customer wants, and by extension, helps the entrepreneur, you, figure out what to Build.

"

Discovery is about being open to all ideas and listening in strange places.

RESOURCES

A big part of finding a killer idea worth pursuing is delineating the resources necessary to make it happen, meaning that you have all the skills and resources to bring the product to market and the ability to sell it. The resources needed consist of both *physical* and *skill* resources.

In order to build an on-line birdhouse business, for example, you need the following physical resources: wood, a hammer, nails, and saw. You also need the following skill resources: basic measurement and ratio mathematics, design plans, sawing, and hammering. In order to sell the birdhouse you need skills in communications and marketing; you might even want to incorporate web development and photography, just to name a few. As an entrepreneur, it is imperative that you learn to map out all the resources it will take to execute on a new venture.

Money is a critical resource that receives a lot of entrepreneurial focus. The only reason you need money is to gain resources you do not currently possess.

For example, if you do not have the hammer needed to build your birdhouse you may need buy one. Likewise, if you do not have the skills to hammer then you will need to hire someone who can, which requires money.

This may sound like a no brainer, but what happens if you cannot gather the money to get the resources you do not have access to? What will you do then?

You have a few options. You could make or borrow the physical resources needed or you could learn the skills needed.

Keep in mind your main objective, as an entrepreneur, is to maximize your access to available resources. Look for ways to acquire the resources you need without spending money, but do not be afraid to hire when your skills are lacking. Just because you "can" does not mean you should. Too often, someone will do something 80% when the business requires something to be done at 100%.

Fortunately, there are two ways to help you develop your understanding of the resources you have available to you in the Discover Phase as they are related to your idea. The Idea Evaluation Form and the Entrepreneur Skills Assessment Form are tools that help highlight areas that either your idea is missing or you, as a founder, are missing.

Idea Evaluation Form:

timlcooley.com/idea-evaluation-form

Skills Assessment Form:

timlcooley.com/entrepreneur-skill-assessment-form

One of the top reason for business failure is an inability to acquire a needed resource. Your job is to figure out what all those needed resources are, whether or not you have them, what it would take to acquire them or if you need to learn them. If, at any point, you cannot obtain the resources, kill the idea.

"

Money is a means to gain access to a resource you do not currently possess. If, at any point you cannot obtain a resource, kill the idea.

"

CUSTOMERS

Customers are the entity who actually spends money on the goods and services we are selling. They are the lifeblood of any business. Never forget: you are building your idea *for them,* not for yourself. To that end, it is imperative to know who our customers are and the steps it will take to get them to buy the product or service. Do the research! Spend time getting to know them.

The easiest type of business to gain customers are typically Business to Business style companies (B2B). Usually, B2B businesses respond to Functional and Economical Value at a higher rate than Business to Consumer (B2C) businesses. This make selling a bit easier. Business to Consumer endeavors B2C can be a lot more difficult and require a much deeper understanding of buying behavior to obtain sales. Other business models exist and get more complex; for example, selling a medical device or trying to get reimbursed via health insurance can be extremely difficult and require a large amount of industry specific knowledge and connections.

The key to customers is knowing *who* is going to buy. Often, an entrepreneur actually has a killer idea, but does not have an "in" which enables them to sell directly to the buyer, even though the customer needs the product. It is your job to develop connections that will aid in Discovery, Building or Testing the idea out. Find out who the person paying, is!

EXAMPLES

Hat Display – I worked with a person who created a hat display because they had hundreds of hats sitting in their closet, and wanted a unique way to show them off at home. He spent $100,000 building a product, but did not spend any time trying to figure out how to get the product to the customer. He had no money left over for marketing. Ultimately, he now has a garage full of the product and no idea how to sell them.

Fitness App - I worked with a person who was in the process of developing a fitness-tracking app. The app had many interesting features and successfully helped customers lose weight, but the challenge was monetization. Who was going to pay for it;iInsurance companies, employers, hospitals, clinics or the person using the app? If you do not know much about the health industry and do not have connections in this space, targeting the right buyer can be extremely difficult, even though your product or service is effective and available.

"

Customers are the people who actually spend money on the things we create.

"

SALES

Believe it or not, many entrepreneurs actually overlook planning out how to make a sale. My first business failed for many reasons, but the nail in the coffin was that we could never actually accept the customers payment. We believed we had a good idea. We spent years developing the skills we needed to make the business work. We had working technology and then went to integrate the payment portal and it would not work. Payment integration is relatively easy now, but not when we started that project. Our team could not overcome this resource barrier, so we changed directions with the company, ultimately turning it into a profitable venture.

Companies like VenMo, Stripe, PayPal, Square, and Shopify have made taking payments from consumers easy, but getting your product in front of those consumers at the right time with the right message has never been more difficult. Forty years ago there were only a few ways a company could promote a product. Companies needed to have their marketing messaging in the single newspaper, on one of a few TV stations or have it available in a major box store like Sears or JC Penney's. Currently, there is so much competition for consumer attention. If you do not have a strategy for connecting your product to your customer at the right time, it is drastically less likely to make any meaningful sales. You need to know what to say, when to say it and how to say it to maximize your opportunity.

If you are selling an expensive wedding gift, would it be better to sell it online, at a farmers' market, or partnering with a wedding venue? It may seem like this is an easy question to answer, but think about each option. The farmer's market is not targeted, but it is easy to set up a booth and easy to take payment. Online stores are more complicated to set up, but you can be detailed in your targeting. A wedding venue seems more targeted, but you need to make an arrangement with the venue and may lose some of your profit--they aren't going to let you have something for nothing. There are many more avenues to sell a product: Amazon, Etsy, and wedding conventions are great options; however, you still need to develop the skills needed to make those a viable sales channels. The takeaway is this: Clearly defining the channel of product delivery to the customer is another area to *Discover*.

"

There is so much competition for customers' attention. If you do not have a strategy connecting your product to your customers at the right time, it becomes drastically less likely you will make meaningful sales.

EXERCISE

We are going to start a lemonade beverage company together.
Lemonade
Idea: Lemonade Company

Problem: Thirst

Value:
Economical: ??
Functional: We use real sugar and lemons sourced from local growers.
Psychological: Proceeds go to helping veterans.
Social: ??

Note: Labeling the product with *real* add to not only the functional value (what it is made with), but is also adds to psychological and social. It makes you feel good that it isn't just chemicals and when you tell people about it, they give you social credit.

What recipe would we use?
Should our container be aluminum, glass or plastic?
What do we need to know in order to make this decision?

How would we manufacture the lemonade if we need to make 10,000 bottles?

How much would it cost to build a booth?

Is there more value we can add?

Customer

Who drinks lemonade? When do they drink it? Why lemonade instead of other beverages?

Sales

Does it need to be at baseball games, sold at a fair or farmers' market or a booth on the corner of my street?

Clearly, this is not an exhaustive list of questions, but each answer starts us down a path that opens new lines of questioning. What other questions did you come up with?

KILLING THE IDEA

Remember, we are not actually building anything in the Discover step; we are Discovering physical and skill-based resources we'd require in order to Build in the *next* step, as well as analyzing who might buy a product and how we might get it in their hands.

Most ideas evolve over time. It is possible to begin with a viable idea that seems realistic to build, but as the market's needs evolve you may find, a new skill is required or that you do not have access to a specific resource needed to continue. This is why the *Discover* step is so important. As an entrepreneur, you are trying to identify potential pitfalls as early as possible. Do not underestimate the importance of Discovery. Discovery is where truly *killer ideas* are found.

Many great entrepreneurs spend a lot of time and money to Build an idea only to realize they never had access to the one resource they needed to make the business work. Equally, they never spent the time required to solve the issue before setting out to Build the idea. I have seen many otherwise smart and capable entrepreneurs end up extremely broke and down hearted.

If you keep running into roadblocks when trying to acquire a certain resource, focus on acquiring the resource over everything else. It will not matter if you can achieve ninety percent of your other goals if this one key resource is missing; you must solve this issue before moving on. If you have done this step correctly, you are truly on your way to creating a killer idea. Many entrepreneurs will skip over vital parts of this step and will not delve deeply enough into the whole process to actually *Discover* what the product needs. If you have not done so already, spend time on these tools so that they can help you Discover what resources you may be missing and which might, ultimately, prevent your idea from being a success.

STEP 3: BUILD

We have done enough thinking, and now it's time to *Build*. We have to get the idea out of our head and show it to someone else--preferably your ideal customer. You will want to start by Building the **Minimum Viable Product (MVP)** in order to solicit important feedback.

This feedback process is one of the first forms of *Validation*. I will say it here, but it will come back in the Test phase. "The only validation that matters is sales." However, you need to be building the right product for the right customers. You may have to spend some money on this these early versions, but not as much as you might think. It is important to spend as little, but adequate, money on, what is still at this stage only a *good* idea in order to find if it is a killer idea.

Many early entrepreneurs like the thrill of Building over the grind of selling, so they get stuck in a loop of making things and not finding someone who wants to buy it. The truth is, they just have not spent enough time Discovering what their product or service requires to actually sell. Also, keep in mind;

we are only in the *Build* phase because we believe
we may have a killer idea.

MINIMUM VIABLE PRODUCT (MVP)

An MVP is a tangible representation of your idea. It can take many forms, but the simplest version is drawing it on paper.

Depending on the idea, your MVP can be simple or complex. Your goal is to get to sales (Test) as fast as possible. As long as you keep the "What do I need to Build in order to Test my sales process" mindset, you will make better and cheaper decisions when it comes to making your MVP.

There are only four company types: service companies, physical product companies, software companies, and pleasure companies. All businesses are one of these types, or a combination of them. For example, Nintendo employs a combination of all of these approaches. (Service: They provide ongoing support and games through their software platform; Physical Product: The Switch, games and controllers are all physical products; Software: The games and the platform are all built with software; Pleasure: They create their own games which are fun.)

The more company types required for your business idea to function successfully, the more complex your MVP will be to Test, which can be expensive. A killer business is one you can completely execute. If this is your first venture, it's best to start off with one company type and then add more as the product or service grows. Should you have access to all the resources you need try to build the most effective, compelling MVP you can.

SERVICES

A service company is any company that sells a *skill*. Examples include consulting, digital marketing, lawn mowing, cleaning, IT support, animation, art, and lead generation. There are hundreds of services that you could do for other people. Some skills can be learned very quickly, such as basic landscaping, while others take years to develop, such as becoming the head of a commercial construction operation. Service industries are the easiest to develop. If you have a skill, go out and get your first client to pay you for it.

I am oversimplifying the process of acquiring customers and, by extension, making sales, but if you spent adequate time Discovering your customer, you should have a good idea of how to present enough value that they become willing to pay for your services.

There is one major problem I have seen with early stage service-based companies, which has to do with their sales cycles. These service businesses often go through cycles during which only little commerce comes through the door, followed by cycles in which too much comes through and demand cannot be met. This is commonly referred to as *feast or famine*. Figuring out how you will overcome this (or avoid it to begin with) should be part of the Discover step.

"

A service company is any company where you sell a skill or knowledge you have.

PHYSICAL PRODUCTS

When it comes to physical products, it is important to show, not tell. It is imperative to get your idea out of your head and into your customers' hands. Usually, the first MVP of your product is a conceptual drawing. Do not be afraid to show off your idea. You need to get feedback!

There is no way to tell what your next MVP may look like. Do not just jump straight to 3D printing, (even though it is cool!). You could carve the idea out of wood or cut apart aluminum cans and Build a model. You could take an existing product and spray paint it to look like the product you want to sell. You can Photoshop pieces of existing products together to get closer to your idea. Get creative here, because the more time and effort you spend Building your MVP, the better information and feedback you are likely to receive from customers.

Do not skip this step; it is very important. Even if you want to go the 3D printing route, I would still encourage you to build a faux version first. All you need to do is convey the concept. Remember, the goal is to see if your idea is killer.

"

Show. Do not tell. Get your product out of your head and into your customers' hands.

"

SOFTWARE

Everyone has an idea for a super cool app or some type of software. If you are going down the app route and you have made it to the Build step, then either you can code it or you have enough money to pay a developer who can. You should already know app development is extremely expensive. In either case, your first version MVP is a wire-frame mock-up. You need to show what the app or software is supposed to do.

My personal favorite mock-up tool is Power Point. I have used Power Point to design layouts for highly complicated software as well as mobile games. Software mock-ups, not only show what your product does, but also how a user will interact with it.

"

A Minimum Viable Product for all software is a wireframe mock-up.

"

PLEASURE

Pleasure is one of the hardest services to provide MVPs. While you make many iterations on the idea, often you have to release a "final" version and hope that works.

BOOKS

A book can only come out once. There are opportunities to republish newer editions later, but typically, a book is a one-and-done type of business.

MOVIES

The MVP for a movie is a script. It may start even earlier as a story. The next MVP is likely to be storyboards. It is possible to make multiple revisions of the story, but you cannot make changes to a movie after it is done.

ART

Art, paintings, drawings, pottery, etc., is a one and done type of business. There really is not an MVP other than the final product.

VIDEO GAMES

Video games follow similar principles to software and products. The first version of the game can be made with paper, known as a paper prototype. This version gives a feel for the game, but it cannot mimic the logic or speed provided by the software. This type of mockup can help gauge and chart the User Interface, or UI, but again does not help communicate the feeling of the game. The next step is a white box, which is a playable version of the game that allows you to test the mechanics of the game. Fortunately, mobile games and web-based games are easily updated.

EVENTS

Events such as weddings, sporting events, athletic leagues, fundraisers and anything that requires getting a group of people to do something are difficult to MVP. Usually you need to just do it and make it happen. Then you build on the first one. Technically the first one is the MVP, even though it is actually a final version.

❝

A pleasure type business is one of the hardest businesses to create an MVP.

❞

EXERCISE

Let us build an MVP version of Tinder. Tinder is a dating app where a person can choose whether they are interested in meeting a potential partner. Its interface is simple: swipe right if you like someone, or swipe left if you do not. This is over simplifying the product. There is more to the product now. For now, let us focus on its core feature.

How would you build an MVP of this without using any code?
How could you get someone to pay you to provide a similar experience?

Here is how I would have done it:

1) Collect images of men and women who are roughly the same age and single.
2) Ask the potential user to examine each picture, placing the photos they like on the right and the ones they do not on the left.
3) Track user results using Google Sheets.
4) Use the data to match potential partners.
5) Charge users to know with whom they matched.

This may not work, but I would know quickly if my assumption, "Will a customer pay to know who they matched with and if so, how much?" was a viable business.

KILLING THE IDEA

Remember, your goal is to Build the MINIMUM viable product. You want to do the least amount you can to convey your idea.

- If you do not want to share your idea, kill the idea.
- If you cannot build a faux version of your idea, kill the idea.
- If you cannot figure out a way to demonstrate your idea, kill the idea.

You are going to be spending a lot of time and money on this idea. You want to do everything in your power to know if the idea is killer, not just good. This is why you need to Test your idea once you learn how to Build the first version.

STEP 4: TEST

Everything you have done so far has been completed in order to answer one question, "Will a customer buy this?"

What we need to do now is create the Minimum Viable Business (MVB). MVB is defined as the least amount of resources and effort required to actually sell.

There is a common misconception that you have to Build the final version of your idea in order to sell it. This is not true. You only need to Build just enough of the idea to get to a sale. Remember, I stated this earlier, "the only validation that matters is sales." I will be giving ideas on how to Test your MVB for all four-company types.

"

You need to Build just enough of the idea to get a sale. 'The only validation that matters is sales.'

SERVICE INDUSTRY

Service industries are the easiest to Test. Many service businesses are cash-based, such as cleaning and lawn care. This means you just need to get clients. You do not even have to build a website, or provide a credit card processing system. You can just get started and take cash for payment.

With some services, it can be a bit more complicated to find your ideal customers. Life coaching, business coaching and consulting take a different type of customer Discovery process and may require you to build more credibility in order to actually sell the service.

Keep in mind that every service industry requires the need to prove that you are capable. You, the person doing the service, are the value. You are the Social value of your business. Most people will buy your service because they have seen your work before, know your reputation or know you and select you over others.

If you aren't completely sure about the value you can provide, which is common at the beginning of a venture, then and only then should you provide your service for free in order to build up your portfolio. However, do your best to get paid, even if it is $1.

"

Service industries are the easiest to Test. Start off as a cash only business. If you are just getting started, charge at least $1 to perform your service.

"

SOFTWARE

It is nearly impossible to use your software MVP to get sales in software; most of the time, an entrepreneur will need a working version of the software to gain sales. However, what you can do is break the software into pieces and Test each one to see where the value is. Consider:

1) What information do you need to gather?
2) What has to happen with that information?
3) What is your consumer hoping to gain with that information?

Each one of these steps can be completed manually until you get your first sale then use software to phase yourself out. For example, assume you have a long onboarding process with your software. You know it is possible to automate this, but for your first 100 sales, you might have to do it manually. Go get the sales first and then start to phase yourself out as you now have the money to automate the onboarding process.

APPLICATIONS

An application is a specialized piece of software that performs a task, like a calculator or a fitness tracker. These applications typically enhance a service you are already using, such as Excel or PowerPoint, which are huge applications and require a lot of development to Test.

Imagine trying to compete with Excel as a spreadsheet.
What core features would you need?
How much would it cost in time to develop?
What would it take to sell it?
Would all of that be worth it?

These types of questions need to be addressed in the Discover phase.

SOFTWARE AS A SERVICE (SAAS)

Many software companies are known as SAAS companies. These types of companies can be Tested very similarly to normal service companies. It is possible to Test your idea without coding, you just have to perform the functions as if you were the computer.

If you think back to the "Tinder" example, we became the matching system. Let us assume people were paying us to find them matches based off our simple experiment. The next thing we could do is develop a way to get more photos into the platform. We are still being paid manually, but now we have more photos for our customers. Next, we may want to develop a way for the people to pay on-line. We are still monitoring the matches manually and reaching out to our clients. This process lets you slowly test/build your MVP.

This process is difficult to actualize, but it helps set priorities in development and it helps refine what needs to be built next.

FREEMIUM

Freemium business models entail offering a service for free with the intention on monetizing another service later. Unfortunately, they are not compatible with the style of Testing I am talking about. What you can do, though, is learn what core features you need through your MVP and Discover additional features that a prospective customer may pay for. You will have to build out a rather large portion of your idea, which can be expensive, so make sure you know what to Build in order for your Test to work.

"

SAAS industries can be tested without coding; you just have to get creative in your approach.

PLEASURE

When it comes to pleasure businesses, such as books and films, most require a completely finished product to actually know if it is going to sell. However, there are other things you can do in order to Test your ability to "sell." One way to Test a pleasure business is to build up an audience. Building an audience takes a lot of work, but if done correctly you will already have a base of support to whom you can sell when the time is right. I heard recently of a group of filmmakers who, instead of releasing their full two-hour movie, decided to launch it in 10-minute increments on YouTube, just to build an audience.

EXAMPLE

Exploding Kittens is a fairly simple card game that raised over $10M using Kickstarter, an online crowdfunding platform where people with ideas can raise money to fund business ventures. The average board game raises around $20,000. Why was this one so much more successful? The creators were the founders of the website The Oatmeal, a satirical comics website, who already had a following of millions users. Before you put the effort into making your product, build your audience. This is your Test.

PHYSICAL PRODUCTS

This is my favorite business type to test. There are so many ways to see if someone will buy your product. Here are three real ways to test a physical product:

1) Boothing
2) Ads + Website
3) Crowdfunding

The best, and I mean the best, thing about a physical product is that you can get to an MVB without the product even working! You will see how this is possible in the Plus Five example later in the book.

MAKE ON DEMAND

One way to Test your product is to only make it once it has been ordered. This process is known as Make On Demand. One of the benefits of a make on demand product is the need to carry little to no inventory. A smoothie is a good example of a make on demand business model; you do not make the smoothie until it is ordered.

Many young entrepreneurs start their business ventures with the humble lemonade stand. The lemonade stand of the eCommerce world is a t-shirt company. Many t-shirt companies start as on-demand businesses just to test if there is a market for their idea. Once they have proven there is a market that can start to buy shirts in quantities that make the margins on the shirts much more exciting.

If you are looking to do e-commerce, I highly recommend trying out online sales with a t-shirt company, you will learn a lot.

BOOTHING

Boothing is a great way to Test this type of product or service delivery. If you have ever been to a farmers' market, the people who are selling their goods are boothing. Booths can range in cost, so find a cheap one. One company I worked with went to a farmers' market with a prototype. They used that prototype to gather email addresses for potential customers. Once they had what they felt was a good enough list, then they launched a crowd funding campaign. Their campaign and product were successful because of this strategy.

You could also do presales at these events or make the product for the customer once you get home or to the office.

When boothing, make sure you choose a venue where your ideal customers will be. For example, if you are selling a product for teachers, a farmers market might not be the best place to test it. The farmers market may not have enough teachers present to know if your product is going to sell properly.

ADS + WEBSITE

This is my favorite way to test products. Later in the book, I will show you how I did this with Our First Quilt. The idea is to build a website, using fake pictures (or pictures that look close enough to the real thing that a buyer would not really notice) then run ads to that website in order to test marketing conversion rates. Knowing these rates is supercritical when it comes to understanding how to acquire a customer, which is why I like it the best.

Here are the steps:

1) Build a website using Shopify or some other eCommerce platform.
2) Use your MVP you created in Build as the product you are going to sell.
3) Create a "funnel" which leads straight to a buy page; no fluff.

Keep these super simple. You do not need to spend a lot of time or money on these e-commerce platforms. All you need is a "Buy" button to be able to track the conversions.

Google and Facebook ads are the easiest tools to use to get data for validation, so I strongly advocate you learn them. I will not be going into detail on how to set up an ad, but what you can gain from using them to sell your product before it is made is invaluable.

I have more information on this topic in some of my courses: timlcooley.com/courses

FACEBOOK

Facebook uses complex algorithms to suggest products that I might like based on factors such as my "friends" like it.

I am a fan of Facebook. I mainly use the platform to learn about new things. Every time I open the application, I hope my friends are sharing a cool event, an exciting video or a new product or service I do not know about. As with most things, if my friends like it, the odds are I will like it. This is the basis for how Facebook works. I call this correlation marketing. A correlation is a mutual relationship or connection between two or more things.

"

Use Facebook Ads to create product awareness, with the hope of sales.

"

EXAMPLE

Let us assume we are selling a cat charm bracelet. We need to find people who have the highest likelihood of buying. Our first group would people who like cats and our second would be people whom like charms/bracelets.

Cats
- Meow Mix - cat food
- Fancy Feast - cat food

People who *really* like cats will "like" and "follow" cat food companies on Facebook. Therefore, we can assume these people have a probability of being potential customers.

Charms
- Alex and Ani
- Pandora

People who follow these brands are, again, likely to be interested in the product.

If we combine these two groups in a Venn diagram, the overlap gives us the highest correlation that people will find our product interesting enough to click on it or buy it. This is our demographic.

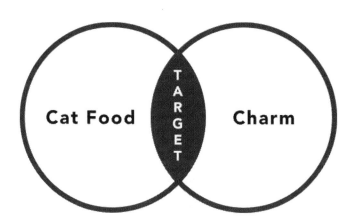

Keep in mind that a Facebook algorithm (pixel) gets better over time. If you are starting cold (no contact list, emails or primed pixel), sales out of the gate are not normal.

GOOGLE ADS

As with Facebook, think about how you use Google.

IMG Search: How to make a birdhouse

If you are like me, when you Google something, you are hoping the results are the best answer to your question. If the first result does not give you an answer, you move on. Using Google Ads, you can influence the answer consumers receive. By understanding how to use the Keyword Planner, you can make assumptions about what people are looking up, and you can take advantage of an opportunity to display an ad that can answer their question.

People who search on Google are one-step closer to purchasing than they are with Facebook ads. They came to your website with the intent on doing some sort of action. We hope that action is buying.

"

Google ads are for answering searches. You want to answer your customers question with your products ad.

"

FUNNEL

You are testing conversions. You will want to set up a funnel. A funnel means you want to see how many people convert to a sale. In our example, a sale means the customer actually clicked the buy button. What you want to know is: how many people saw the ad, and how many of those people followed all the way through to a click on the buy button? This tactic is not about making money, but understanding if your product will make money.

Funnel Example

Imagine you spent $100 on an ad.
100,000 saw the ad, impressions. (top of the funnel)
1000 people clicked on that ad.
 5 people clicked on your buy button. (bottom of the funnel)

Is your funnel profitable? It depends on the price of the product you are selling and the margins you have, so run the numbers. You can also run this funnel in reverse. You can make assumptions about the click-through rate (CTR) and work backward. This is actually good to practice. Use 1% CTR from the top of the funnel to the bottom as your base; the results may shock you!

CROWD FUNDING

Crowdfunding is a common source of raising capital and proving a market exists for a product or service. Many of the Test ideas I have mentioned above should be done prior to launching a crowdfunding campaign. Having run and worked with multiple crowdfunding campaigns, just putting a campaign out there without a plan will not work. Think of a crowdfunding campaign as a product launch; you need a strategy to be successful. One concept I have heard that works really well is to get 500 committed people to back you the day it goes live, odds are you will reach your goal with that many people.

You should be much further into product development before you undertake a crowdfunding campaign, but it is possible to make a fake product and run a crowdfunding campaign with it. I do not recommend this as an action, but if it helps you get started then make it happen!

KILLING THE IDEA

The Test is the culmination of everything that we have discussed previously. If by now you have sales, clearly this is a killer idea!

If you cannot figure out how to sell your product, nothing else matters, so kill the idea.

Throughout the development of your idea, you should be Testing it, especially during the Create and Build steps. We naturally want to create things. We find happiness in Building. Most early entrepreneurs struggle to sell. It is the most uncomfortable part of getting started. If you cannot find a way to prove there is a market by doing the sales work yourself or hiring someone else to do it for you, kill the idea. The Test is the second half of a killer idea. Remember a killer idea is one a customer feels is worth paying for.

Do not be too quick to kill the idea in the Test stage, sometimes it takes different approaches and some luck to find the people who find your idea worth paying for. If one way does not work, get creative to Discover a new one. A friend of mine sells jewelry. Naturally, she thought she should put her product in stores where jewelry was sold. After a few months of experiments, she was not getting the sales she expected. She reached out to a friend who owned a cookie store, who let her put the product in the store to test if sales would increase. By using her resources, she was able to find a unique way to find customers where there was no competition. Sometimes you just have to get creative when it comes to sales!

KILLER IDEA

Congratulations, you have learned the four step process to finding a killer idea: Create, Discover, Build and Test.

A Killer Idea is:
1) An idea you can completely bring to market.
2) An idea that a customer pays for.

To ensure we have the right idea, we have been diligently on the lookout for that one pitfall which, no matter how hard we try, will prevent our success, thus killing our idea. Finding that one thing that will kill your idea is not easy and might be undetectable until you move further through the development process.

NEXT STEPS

What should I do if I killed my idea?

Please remember that all of your ideas are good, we want to find the killer ones! Just because you killed, an idea does not mean you cannot work on it. I am just suggesting to not putting a significant amount of time or money into it. If the Idea Evaluation Form has determined there are some major gaps you need to fix in order to make the idea killer, this is a good. The goal of the evaluation form is to help identify areas you should focus on.

Idea Evaluation Form:

timlcooley.com/idea-evaluation-form

Once you have identified the gaps, you have two options: option one; you can change what it is you are doing, but stay in the market you are targeting. Maybe there is a product you could sell that is smaller in scope than your current idea. Try to build the new product with the resources you can access and leverage. Option two; leave the idea in the Discovery phase. If the concept keeps coming back to you and you keep learning about it, maybe you will discover the missing resources over time.

Keep a running list of all your good ideas. This will help you come up with more and more good ideas that you can evaluate to find a killer one.

What should I do after I get a sale?

First congratulations on your sale, not many ideas make it this far! This is a big deal and you need to be proud of your accomplishments. However, you are not done yet. The real fun is just beginning. Now you need to be able to repeat the sales process to have a successful business. Keep in mind, every time you make a sale it is a Test. The sale should inform decisions you make to get the next sale.

You have a killer idea. You now just need to figure out how to get repeated sales.

MY EXAMPLES

I have killed many ideas; some went all the way through the process into full development, while others never made it past the Create phase. I promise you, the more time you spend challenging your own assumptions the better off you will be in the end.

This next section talks about a few products I have worked on which used my process. Imagine these ideas are yours: what would you do differently if you took them through my process? Think about all the resources you currently have access to; could you make the ideas Killer or would they be Killed?

COMPUCK

Create

During my MBA program, I took a class in which we had to come up with a new product. The requirements for the product was that it had to fit into the Internet Of Things (IOT) category and it had to use a Rasberry Pi, a computer like device. Those were the only rules.

Good Idea: A device that measures compost and reports details of the compost to a user via a web application.

Problem: People do not actually know how their compost is actually performing. It just sits there.

Value:
Economical: ??
Functional: Composters would know if they needed to add specific nutrients to make the best compost.
Social: Social aspects to an app
Psychological:??

Discover

No one on the team actually had a composter, so there was a lot to discover. This discovery required gaining knowledge from people outside the group. We started with some basic questions:

- How many people compost?
- What measurements are required to understand composting?
- What would happen after you knew this information?
- How would we gather the information?
- Where would we source the sensors?

This is only a sample of the thousands of questions we needed to ask.

Idea Evaluation Form Assessment:

51%

Build

We did not have all of the information needed to Build a working version. We needed user feedback, so we built a non-working MVP to get feedback. We did not completely know all the resources that were needed yet, ether. Using an MVP would could Test viability, would someone actually use it and how would they use it? To see if it was a Killer idea we needed to know, do customers care enough about the idea to make it worth actually Building a working version.

Our first version of the "app" was built in PowerPoint. To demonstrate the device we spray-painted a smoke detector black to mimic what the product might look and feel like.

Total Cost: $20
- Smoke Detector $15
- Paint $5
- App $0

Test

With our "working" device, the black smoke detector, and our "working" app, the Power Point presentation, we gave the product to five different people who were already composting. We watched how they used our device and app. It was cool, because people actually put the device in their compost and played with the app as if the thing was working.

RESULT: KILLED

What we learned from the test.

- Black was the wrong color, it needed to be orange or some other bright color, so when people would stir their compost they would not hit the device.
- Composting for most people was a hobby and not something they took very seriously, even though they were intentional about composting.
- The price point they may be willing to pay was much less than $100, which is what we were expecting.
- It was barely a "nice to have" and definitely not a "need to have".

Next Steps: We decided to kill the idea, because our testers did not really seem excited about the idea. They all used it and thought it would be cool, but there was no real business in it. There was no reason to continue; we did not even finish the IOT project, we did something else completely. Not a killer idea.

PLUS FIVE

Create

I spent about 7 years developing both board and electronic mobile games. During one playtest session, there was also a Magic The Gathering card game tournament. I walked through the tournament and could not help but gasp due to the strong smell of body odor.

Good Idea: Create a deodorant line targeted at competitive card gamers.

Problem: Playing board and video games can take a long time to play, hours. Games are stressful and create sweat. Sweat that is stationary starts to smell due to bacteria.

Value:
Economical: Deodorant would be located at the game stores for convenience. Price point would have to be close to "normal" deodorant.
Functional: Stop sweat or masks the odor.
Social: Not smelling in front of your friends. Not getting kicked out of the board game store for odor.
Psychological: There would be an association to other gamers.

Discover

I needed to know if odor from gamers was a real problem. I reached out to a number of board game stores. A few of them sent back pictures of signs they had posted, "We reserve the right to kick you out if you smell." Unbelievably, this was at many board game places. I decided to go further.

- How do you make deodorant?
- How does deodorant actually work?
- Is aluminum bad for you?
- Where do you produce deodorant?
- What are the MOQs (minimum order quantities)?
- Why do gamers not wear deodorant? (this was an assumption)
- What is a gamer?

Idea Evaluation Form Assessment:

80%

Build

This was actually easy to Build. Deodorant already exists. I learned from ComPuck I could mock up an example, "fake one", for cheap.

I was a big gamer, so I drew inspiration from games I played. I knew the colors had to be recognizable or at least play off the fantasy theme. I chose orange to represent a legendary item, like the ones in games. The branding had to look like a playing card.

To fake one, I bought a bunch of Old Spice deodorants and removed all their labeling. I found an orange spray paint that closely matched what I wanted and spray-painted them.

I hired an artist to design a logo and labeling. After a few trips to Kinkos for stickers, I had a version of the deodorant I could Test.

Total Cost: $500
- Video $200
- Deodorant $50
- Logo $100
- Paint $5
- Advertising $145

Test

During the Discover phase, I learned that my minimum order quantity (MOQ) was around 10,000 unit to have it made in the US. This would have roughly cost me $15,000.

I used the fake product to put together a few product shots and videos and I took all of that to Kickstarter. I had manufacturing all lined up and ready for production, but I needed to know whether people would buy it.

I used my knowledge of online marketing and Kickstarter and off we were to Test the market.

RESULT: KILLED

What I learned from the test.

- Gamers were extremely upset. "Why not use 'normal' deodorant."
- Board game stores loved it; every shop I reached out to bought it.
- Price matters on Kickstarter. A $4 product needs a lot of backers in order to hit $25,000
- My messaging was mixed. The product, video and messaging targeted different demographics of gamers.

Next Steps: I decided that I would need to market the product differently. Raising that type of capital on Kickstarter was not the right way to go about this product. If the MOQ was smaller, say 1000, I would have had enough resources to actually move forward, but with a minimum need of $15,000 it exceeded the allotted budget for the project.

Even though this product scored high on the Idea Evaluation Form, the information gathered in the Discover and Test steps proved enough to not move forward with the project.

Not a killer idea.

OUR FIRST QUILT

(COLORING QUILT)

Create

During the summer of my MBA program, some friends and I wanted to start a company. We had a huge list of ideas. The idea of doing something in the wedding industry appealed to us, and one of the founders liked the idea of wedding invitations.

Good Idea: Create a custom wedding quilt that resembled a wedding invitation.

Problem: Wedding memorabilia.

Value:
Economical: None to speak of.
Functional: ??
Social: It would be cool to have hanging in your house, like an heirloom
Psychological: ??

Discover

We had a decent idea, but honestly had no idea how to make a quilt.

- How do you make a quilt?
- How would we get the pattern onto the quilt?
- How would we make that pattern customizable?
- Who do you sell this to?
- What is batting?
- Embroider, Paint, Quilt?
- What could we charge?

Idea Evaluation Form Assessment:

81%

Build

We wanted to fake this process as well. We had no idea how to make a quilt, so to Build our first MVP we commissioned an artist on Fivver from Spain. We took his drawing and printed out 60 sheets of paper, taped them together, and took multiple photos. A few Photoshop tricks later and we had our first version on the quilt.

We built a website, using Shopify, to sell the quilt.

We now had a few product photos to show people and were able to go to some local quilt shops, print shops and custom design firms to get quotes on what it would cost to have someone else produce the product for us. The price came back at over $1000 to produce each quilt.

We felt like we could do a Make On Demand type business, so if we could just sell one we could make it with the proceeds.

Total Cost: $100

Test

Our Test was simple. Just leave the website up and see if anyone would buy. We could have run ads to it, but we wanted to see if any natural traffic would exist. This was a super low budget Test. The test consisted of just leaving the website up and hoping something would happen.

It worked! We had a woman from Australia "buy" one. We ultimately canceled the order, but it was a real purchase.

RESULT: KILLER IDEA

What I learned from the test.
1) We should make them. Someone wanted to buy.
2) Even though we had a sale, the time to produce (close to three days) and the price was way too high to have the volume we wanted.
3) No one on our team knew how to quilt, so it was not really worth the effort.

Next Steps: We decided to shelf the idea. It was not killed; it just was not possible at the time. My co-founder learned to quilt. We felt that was necessary to make the product real. In the meantime, we kept looking for ways to make the product work. Embroidery was too expensive and would take too long. We tried painting it, but the paint and stencil did not make it look good. Another idea was to do emulsion printing, which might have looked good, but felt cheap. Ultimately, we found the right tool to do the job, bought it and went back to Test the market.

This product actually evolved over time. While testing the wedding quilt market we discovered some valuable insight from a vendor. The co-founder quilted the logo for the company (in colors) and hung it next to the Our First Quilt wedding quilt. A DJ asked why we did not color the wedding quilt. This simple question led us to our next experiment. We took a similar product to a wedding show and let the guests color the quilt. Their response was so much better. We decide at that point to switch the product to Coloring Quilt, which is a Killer Idea.

www.ourfirstquilt.com

CONCLUSION

I hope you have a better idea of what a good idea is versus what is a killer idea.

A killer idea is an idea:

1) You completely bring the idea to market with the resources you have.
2) You find someone who is willing to pay for it.

You now know the four steps needed to find a killer idea:

Create: Find an idea where you can create a ton of value.

Discover: Discover all the skill and physical resources needed to bring this product or service to market.

Build: Make a facsimile or prototype that enables you to illustrate your ideas to others.

Test: Use your prototype for market research to ascertain whether or not consumers will purchase it.

Throughout my process, you are trying to determine if the idea should be killed or continues to be killer.

I have given you some solid examples of how I used my process to Create, Discover, Build, Test and Kill an idea to determine which ideas were killer and which ones ultimately stayed as "good". I hope you use some of the tools I have mentioned to discover your resources and how they help define the idea.

Idea Assessment Form

timlcooley.com/idea-evaluation-form

Entrepreneur Skill Assessment Form

timlcooley.com/entrepreneur-skill-assessment-form

I would love to hear stories about ideas you have killed and ones that you are continuing to pursue.

Share your story with us at timlcooley.com.

Get out there and start finding your Killer Idea!

Made in the USA
San Bernardino, CA
25 July 2019